Crested Gecko as Pets

Caring For Your Crested Geckos

Crested Gecko Facts, Caresheet, Breeding, Nutritional information, Husbandry and Housing Tips, and So Much More!

By Lolly Brown

Copyrights and Trademarks

All rights reserved. No part of this book may be reproduced or transformed in any form or by any means, graphic, electronic, or mechanical, including photocopying, recording, taping, or by any information storage retrieval system, without the written permission of the author.

This publication is Copyright ©2019 NRB Publishing, an imprint. Nevada. All products, graphics, publications, software and services mentioned and recommended in this publication are protected by trademarks. In such instance, all trademarks & copyright belong to the respective owners. For information consult www.NRBpublishing.com

Disclaimer and Legal Notice

This product is not legal, medical, or accounting advice and should not be interpreted in that manner. You need to do your own due-diligence to determine if the content of this product is right for you. While every attempt has been made to verify the information shared in this publication, neither the author, neither publisher, nor the affiliates assume any responsibility for errors, omissions or contrary interpretation of the subject matter herein. Any perceived slights to any specific person(s) or organization(s) are purely unintentional.

We have no control over the nature, content and availability of the web sites listed in this book. The inclusion of any web site links does not necessarily imply a recommendation or endorse the views expressed within them. We take no responsibility for, and will not be liable for, the websites being temporarily unavailable or being removed from the internet.

The accuracy and completeness of information provided herein and opinions stated herein are not guaranteed or warranted to produce any particular results, and the advice and strategies, contained herein may not be suitable for every individual. Neither the author nor the publisher shall be liable for any loss incurred as a consequence of the use and application, directly or indirectly, of any information presented in this work. This publication is designed to provide information in regard to the subject matter covered.

Neither the author nor the publisher assume any responsibility for any errors or omissions, nor do they represent or warrant that the ideas, information, actions, plans, suggestions contained in this book is in all cases accurate. It is the reader's responsibility to find advice before putting anything written in this book into practice. The information in this book is not intended to serve as legal, medical, or accounting advice.

Foreword

Crested geckos are now becoming more popular as reptile household pets. Over the last few years there was an increase among reptile hobbyists who wants to keep these colorful and exotic animals; these animals almost neared extinction in 1994, but fortunately they are now very common as captive pets; gecko breeds in general now comes next to snakes and monitor lizards in terms of popularity. Crested geckos originally came from the New Caledonian islands, which is near Australia. These cute and small lizard species have amazing physical characteristics and color patterns which makes them very attractive pets even for newbie reptile enthusiasts. They have gorgeous eyes, soft skin, and spiny – looking 'crests' that are very cool looking but on top of that they're also quite easy to handle and keep provided that you have a bit of knowledge about them.

Most people think that handling exotic pets like crested geckos are very difficult but we think if you just have the proper knowledge on how to keep one, you'll be an expert in no time! Fortunately, this book can serve as your guide especially when it comes to understanding and keeping your crested geckos. You'll get to learn amazing facts about the, their behaviors, their characteristics and color patterns, how you should feed and care for them and a whole lot more!

Table of Contents

Introduction 1

Welcome to the Colorful World of Crested Geckos! 1

Chapter One: Understanding Crested Geckos 2

    Origin and Distribution 3

    Crested Gecko Description 4

    Quick Facts 6

Chapter Two: Morphs, Colors, and Genetics 8

    Morphs and Patterns of Crested Gecko 9

        Solid – Colored Crested Geckos (No pattern) 9

        Tiger Crested Geckos 10

        Flame Crested Geckos 10

        Harlequin Crested Geckos 11

        Pinstripe Crested Geckos 11

        Dalmatian Crested Gecko 12

        White Spots Pattern 12

    Crested Gecko Colors 12

    Color Patterns 13

        Creamsicle Crested Geckos 13

        Blonde Crested Geckos 13

        Halloween Crested Geckos 14

        Tricolor Crested Geckos 14

Mocha and Cream 14

Cream on Cream 14

Basic Genetics of Crested Geckos 15

Chapter Three: Crested Geckos as Pets 16

Keeping One or More Crested Geckos 17

Costs of Keeping Crested Geckos 18

Expenses Overview 24

Pros and Cons of Keeping Crested Geckos 25

Chapter Four: Acquiring Crested Geckos 28

Tips When Acquiring a Crested Gecko 29

Is it legal to Keep Crested Geckos? 32

CITES Laws for Crested Geckos 32

Keeping Pet Ownership Documents 33

Conservation Issues/ Concerns 34

Tips When Choosing a Reputable Breeder 35

List of Breeders and Rescue Websites 37

Tips When Choosing a Crested Gecko 40

Signs of Healthy Crested Geckos 41

Subject for Second Thoughts! 42

Chapter Five: Housing Needs of Crested Geckos 44

Acclimating New Crested Geckos 45

Habitat Requirements 47

Enclosure Size 48

Heating and Lighting 49

Required Temperature 50

    Housing Needs Checklist 51

Reminders When Cleaning the Enclosure 51

Chapter Six: Nutrition for Your Crested Gecko 54

Commercial Gecko Diet (CGD) 55

Fruits and Live Prey 56

Protein and Supplements 57

Water 58

Feeding Tips for Your Crested Gecko 59

Chapter Seven: Dealing with Your Crested Geckos 62

Crested Gecko Behavior and Interaction 63

How to Handle Your Crested Gecko 63

Crested Gecko Shedding 65

Chapter Eight: Breeding Your Crested Geckos 68

Sexual Maturity and Sexual Dimorphism 69

Breeding Requirements 70

Feeding Your Breeding Cresties 71

Breeding Basics 72

Incubation 74

Chapter Nine: Common Illnesses of Crested Geckos 76

Common Health Problems 77
Chapter Ten: Summary and Care Sheet 90
Glossary of Reptile Terms... 108
Index 120
Photo Credits 126
References 128

Introduction

Welcome to the Colorful World of Crested Geckos!

Crested geckos are one of the coolest looking creatures you can possibly keep especially if you are a reptile enthusiast. They can 'morph' into different colors and even patterns, and their physical attributes are one – of – a – kind, making them perfect for exhibits if that's something you wanted to do especially if you wanted to show them off during reptile conventions. No wonder quite the 'star' among other reptile breed species!

Introduction: Welcome to Colorful World of Crested Geckos

They originated from the islands of New Caledonia around the western pacific, and near Australia. They usually live and are distributed in cool rain forests. Young crested geckos measure around 5 to 6 centimeters while mature adults measure around 20 to 24 centimeters in length. If they are well – fed by their keepers, these colorful spiny – looking creatures can easily reach maturity just after 9 months to a year. Crested geckos in captivity have a lifespan of around 8 to 12 years but can still be longer if you as the keeper can maintain good husbandry.

Usually, crested geckos found in the wild have body patterns in varying shades of brown and grey colors. The good thing about captive breeding is that these small animals now come in a variety of colors and patterns that you can possibly think of! Thanks to the passionate gecko breeders and hobbyists. You can choose different colors of geckos like orange, deep red colors, and yellow. In terms of patterns crested geckos now comes in stripes, spots, and also chevron markings with other few variants.

And since they are also a lizard species, crested geckos possess small scales with a velvety texture. They have a spiny – looking crests formed around in their head area and past the neck area. They possess fringed and round eyes making them quite unique and identifiable from other similar looking lizard species.

Introduction: Welcome to Colorful World of Crested Geckos

Part of being a responsible pet reptile owner is gaining knowledge in everything you can about this breed species including ways on how one should care for it properly. In the next few pages, you will find lots of helpful information about the personality of the crested geckos, how they live, how to deal with them, and how you can properly raise them. This book also includes information about creating the ideal enclosures and proper feeding for your pet geckos as well as tips for breeding and keeping them healthy.

Introduction: Welcome to Colorful World of Crested Geckos

Chapter One: Understanding Crested Geckos

In this chapter you will receive an introduction to the crested gecko breed including some basic facts, origin and distribution, physical characteristics description, some quick facts, and also the various colors that these cool looking creatures can morph into. This information, in combination with the practical information about keeping crested geckos in the next chapter, will help you decide if this is the perfect pet companion for you. These animals are quite small and look easy to handle but they can also be quite 'naughty' at times. Learning about their biological background and characteristics will surely help you to better understand them and be a much more responsible pet keeper.

Chapter One: Understanding Crested Geckos

Origin and Distribution

Crested geckos belong in Kingdom Animalia, Phylum Chordata, Class Reptilia, Order Squamata, Suborder Sauria, Family Gekkonidae, Genus Rhacodactylus, and Species *R. ciliatus*

In order to understand the needs of your captive crested gecko you should first learn how they live in their natural habitats in the wild. As mentioned earlier crested geckos belong to the family of lizards, and were discovered in the low – elevated rainforests in the northeast side of Australia. They usually live in tree canopies around 10 to 50 feet above the forest floor! You can tell that these creatures aren't afraid of heights! They also tend to live in humid and shaded habitats. Most wild crested geckos are not exported for pet trade however; crested geckos in captivity are widely available.

Crested geckos are also known as the "eyelash gecko," and sometimes as the "Barking gecko." They are also distributed in the southern region of the Isle of Pines and Grand Terre which are some of the islands located near Australia. Though collection data was not properly recorded by breeders and gecko hobbyists during the early imports of these creatures, one thing is for sure; they live in tropical rainforests. In New Caledonia where these geckos were

Chapter One: Understanding Crested Geckos

originally distributed, the place is known to have three seasons; cool, warm, and transition season.

The cool season lasts for about 4 months with cooler temperatures and less rainfall. The warm season lasts for about 6 months with obviously a more humid temperatures and lots of rainfall that are associated with tropical cyclones, while the transition season lasts for about 3 months, and this is the period where there's little to no rainfall but with high winds. The significance of this is that, keepers can emulate the warm season found in the crested geckos natural habitat during the summer, and not around November to March.

Crested Gecko Description

- They have a unique appearance because their skin has fine and crested scales, and they are bred for various color patterns and morphs such as tans, yellows, oranges, red, and other dark colors with different patterns like black spots and tiger stripes.

- Crested geckos are arboreal (loves to climb and live on trees). In captivity, they can climb vertical surface materials (with 500,000 setae), and this is because of their unique foot pads.

Chapter One: Understanding Crested Geckos

- Their foot pads have spatula tipped setae. Each of its setae has around 1000 spatulae attached to it which allows them to bond with solid surfaces, and not slip out.

- Crested geckos, and geckos in general also possess double jointed toes which enables them to remove their food pad from the surface they're climbing into just by lifting their foot from the tip inward.

- Their eyes are big, fringed, and looks a lot like eyelashes which are why they earned a nickname of being the "eyelash gecko." They clean their eyes through licking them.

- They don't fight or bite when threatened but they can surely jump a lot!

- Even if crested geckos are easy to handle, it's best that you avoid handling them all the time especially if they are still young and newly acquired.
- Ensure that you handle them properly to avoid stressing the animal out.

Chapter One: Understanding Crested Geckos

Quick Facts

Pedigree: similar to a lizard species

Breed Size: quite small with a relatively long body structure

Length: adult length measures around 4 to 4.5 inches.

Weight: average weight for hatchlings are between 1 ½ grams to 2 grams; for juvenile average is 16 grams; for adult crested geckos average weight 30 to 50 grams (females); 25 grams to 35 grams (males).

Coat Texture: They have a unique appearance because their skin has fine and crested scales

Color: They are bred for various color patterns and morphs such as tans, yellows, oranges, red and other dark colors

Patterns/Markings: has a different pattern like black spots, harlequin, and tiger stripes.

Feet Type: Crested geckos, and geckos in general also possess double jointed toes which enables them to remove their food pad from the surface they're climbing into just by lifting their foot from the tip inward.

Temperament: docile, gentle, friendly, sensitive, delicate

Chapter One: Understanding Crested Geckos

Strangers: handling is not an issue as long as a person knows how to careful handle the gecko without restricting it or squeezing it

Other Pets: can get along with other crested gecko breed with no more than one male in an enclosure. Not advisable to introduce to other house pets.

Exercise Needs: you just need to provide them with branches or perches to climb on since they are arboreal creatures.

Health Conditions: generally healthy but predisposed to common illnesses such as dehydration, Metabolic Bone Disease, respiratory problems, skin burns, impaction, egg binding, floppy tail syndrome, swollen joints, intestinal parasites and other diseases.

Lifespan: average 10 to 12 years; sometimes can last until 15 years or more

Chapter Two: Morphs, Colors, and Genetics

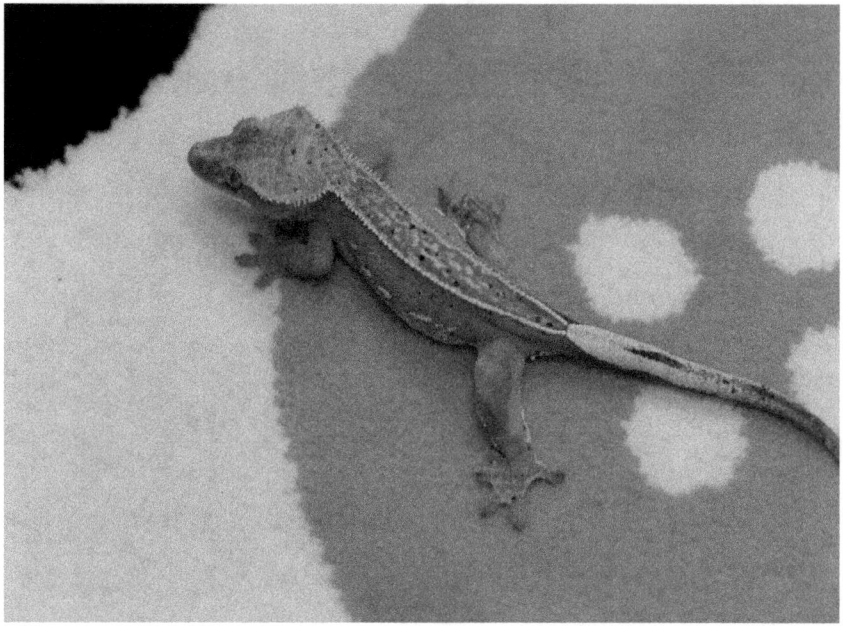

It took many years for experience breeders to develop various colors and patterns in crested geckos. One of the most famous patterns such as dalmatian spots, pinstripe patterns and tiger crested geckos that are now seen in multiple generations. These traits in captive breeds are mostly taken from crested geckos in the wild and we're refined overtime. Polymorphism or commonly known as 'morphs' refers to the presence of the multiple colors/patterns of a species. It also refers to the phenotype (or the observable characteristic) of an animal breed.

Chapter Two: Morphs, Colors, and Genetics

When it comes to crested geckos their morph characteristics are usually inherited as what you're going to learn about in dalmatian spots, pinstripe patterns, and harlequin crested geckos. Get to learn the different variety of colors and patterns as well as the basic genetics of crested geckos in this chapter.

Morphs and Patterns of Crested Gecko

Crested geckos are polymorphic species. This section will cover the different types of morphs and traits in crested geckos.

Solid – Colored Crested Geckos (No pattern)

There are also some crested geckos that don't have a pattern, and only possess a solid color. Solid – colors include the following:

- Olive
- Yellow
- Buckskin
- Chocolate
- Near – black color
- Red
- Orange

Chapter Two: Morphs, Colors, and Genetics

Usually solid – colored crested geckos are what breeders use when breeding colored geckos as they can be used as establish lines. Do take note however, that there's no crested gecko with a full black or white color, they usually come in shades of yellow, red, cream and other existing colors. There are also the so – called bicolor crested geckos that also don't possess any sort of patterns. Bicolor geckos are usually darkish in color or sometimes a lighter color especially at their heads.

Tiger Crested Geckos

Tiger crested geckos also have the same solid – color but this time with stripes. Red tiger crested geckos happen when these creatures are 'fired up,' it occurs when the red pigment overrides or cover the tiger stripes with a dark pattern. On the other hand when yellow tiger crested geckos are much more appealing when they are fired up because of the high contrast.

Flame Crested Geckos

Flame crested geckos can also possess any solid – based color though their dorsal is usually cream colored patterned with minimum pattern. Whiter creams are often more popular and more desirable. On the other hand, chevron crested geckos have flame patterns with a V – shaped pattern on its back. Tiger striped crested geckos can also possess a flame pattern though it usually disappear once they get older.

Harlequin Crested Geckos

Harlequins are crested geckos with high flame patterns. These geckos usually have a base color of either red or near – black with yellow, cream or orange. They also possess this pattern in their limbs. Extreme harlequins are white/ cream patterned crested geckos wherein their body pattern breaks into a sort of creamy dorsal area.

Pinstripe Crested Geckos

Pinstripe pattern is a single and independent characteristic compared to a morph wherein there's a group of traits or specific patterns like flames, harlequin, or tiger. A classic pinstripe usually consists of cream – colored scales with the rest of its back being covered with a flame pattern or a solid cream. A full pinstripe is more desirable compared to a partial pinstripe. Crested geckos that possess pinstripe patterns are usually flames or harlequin but it can also be found in tiger patterned crested geckos.

Dalmatian Crested Gecko

Dalmatian spots in crested geckos are also considered as an independent trait just like pinstripe pattern. Spots can be found in various colors and sizes of crested gecko. Black spots are usually the most common type along with red, white and green spots. Super dalmatian pattern refers to crested geckos with large spots and/ or many spots. Your crested gecko should have at least 100 spots in its body to be qualified as a 'super dalmatian.

White Spots Pattern

White spots among captive breeds had been very common since the early days. It appears as tiny white spots and is usually seen in the gecko's toes, belly, nose, and chest area. However, it can also just be a result of unfinished pigmentation and not something of a genetic trait.

Crested Gecko Colors

Crested geckos can have pigments ranging from very pale to very near – black colors; and from buckskin/ olive colors to red or yellow. Obviously, vibrant color is much more desirable because of its appealing and high contrasts. Extreme light and dark colors are also popular among reptile hobbyists. Crested geckos don't have a blue color/ pattern and this is probably because they lack pigmentation to produce that kind of effect. A blue, purple or even green solid colored crested gecko are highly unlikely. The closest color is olive and sometimes lavender which pretty much a slate grey colored gecko is.

Color Patterns

Creamsicle Crested Geckos

Creamsicle colored geckos have an orange flame pattern. Orange harlequin patterned geckos can also consider a creamsicle. The term creamsicle is usually used for red and cream colored crested geckos.

Blonde Crested Geckos

Blonde crested geckos appear as dark flamed crested geckos (with or without pinstripe patterns). Its dark base color is contrasted with the creamy dorsal. Dark harlequin crested geckos with cream pattern can also be referred to as blonde crested geckos.

Halloween Crested Geckos

These are harlequin patterned crested geckos that possess a dark near – black or orange colored markings. The darker it is, the more vibrant it appears. Black and gold, and black and cream crested geckos also qualify.

Tricolor Crested Geckos

Tricolor crested geckos are basically harlequin geckos with 3 colors. It's quite similar looking to Halloween geckos only with a splash of added cream. Tricolors can also be found in red and yellow crested geckos.

Mocha and Cream

Mocha crested geckos typically possess brown or tan colors with cream markings. They are very appealing if it's in a tiger or reverse pinstripe patterns.

Cream on Cream

This is one of the rarest color combinations of crested geckos. It's basically a light color with a cream dorsal and can often times be seen in tiger flamed patterned geckos.

Chapter Two: Morphs, Colors, and Genetics

Basic Genetics of Crested Geckos

The genetics of the crested geckos are usually masked by a normal appearance. It's quite hard to compare the genetics of crested geckos to other reptiles like leopard geckos and other animal species because the morphs usually work in dominant and recessive genetics. Most of the designer breeds are recessive, and also homozygous. Crested geckos are also polygenic (which means that they have multiple genes that control their phenotype), making them less predictable.

Chapter Three: Crested Geckos as Pets

Crested geckos are cool pets to keep, they are relatively small, easy to handle, and easy to care for. Part of being a responsible keeper is making sure that they are well – kept in the proper surrounding, and be under the right conditions. What you want to do is to replicate their environment in the wild as much as possible so that they can live comfortably in your home as captive – bred house pets. You should also provide for all their basic necessities, and keep them out of harm's way especially if you have other larger reptiles or household pets. In this chapter, you'll learn what it takes in becoming a responsible keeper, and the things you need to acquire in keeping crested geckos.

Chapter Three: Crested Geckos as Pets

Keeping One or More Crested Geckos

Crested geckos can get along with its own breed or with other gecko breed as long as there's no more than one male in an enclosure. Here are some things to keep in mind:

- Make sure there's enough space and vegetation if you're planning to keep two or more crested geckos. Try not to place more than one male crested gecko in an enclosure even if the cage is big. It will stress out the female geckos.

- Provide an adequate living environment

- Ensure that the enclosure is placed in a peaceful surroundings where they can co-exist with other gecko species without being disturbed or threatened by other reptile/ household pets.

- It is not recommended that you introduce them to other household pets. Crested geckos are relatively small creatures, and because of its small size they can always feel threatened. Introducing them to other pets or even being randomly exposed to strangers may not be a good idea.

- As much as possible restrict in handling them if they're still young or if they just recently transferred to their new home. They may feel stress and become lethargic if they are handled too much.

Costs of Keeping Crested Geckos

Crested geckos may be small but like most household pets they still require maintenance which means that you have to provide supplies and be able to cover the needed expenses in order for you to maintain a healthy lifestyle and environment for your pet.

Keeping a crested gecko include those costs that you must cover before you can bring your pet home. Some of the costs you will need to cover include the following:

- Enclosure or cage
- Food and water equipment
- Cleaning supplies
- Cage décor or accessories
- Breeding materials
- Medical care

Chapter Three: Crested Geckos as Pets

In this section you will receive an overview of the expenses associated with purchasing and keeping a crested gecko such as its vivarium, supplements, lighting, watering and veterinary care.

Purchase Price

Purchasing a crested gecko can highly vary depending on the colors and patterns as well as the age and quality of the breed. On average a crested gecko quality will cost around $35 to $100.

29 Gallon Fish Tank/ Reptile Enclosure

This is suited for 3 to 4 crested geckos. Here are some things to keep in mind:

- It must be made out of solid glass/ wood and it should be long enough to create warm and cool side areas

- Generally, the enclosure should be somewhat similar to its natural habitat in the wild, so that it won't have trouble adjusting to its new environment. Providing adequate shelter will make them feel at ease and comfortable as a house pet.

Chapter Three: Crested Geckos as Pets

- In terms of location, they may need to get used to you or other people checking them out while they are inside their enclosure so make sure that the kind of cage you will buy will protect them from any dangerous threats around the house including your house pets.

- Terrarium type enclosures can be quite time consuming in terms of cleaning it, but is still much suitable for your pet gecko because it will provide ample air circulation.

- Glass enclosures might also come in handy during extreme weather conditions or climate for those living in extremely dry or cold countries.

- Of course if you have the time, and you want to save up you can create your own enclosure by copying the style or specs of a cage you like.

Lighting, Heaters, Fixtures:

- Adequate lighting like a 75 watt bulb heat, and under tank heaters or heat pads underneath will provide appropriate temperature and humidity levels inside your pet gecko's cage enclosure.

Chapter Three: Crested Geckos as Pets

- You may also need to purchase things like a UVB bulb though it's not really required as some reptiles can benefit from low levels of UVB light including the crested gecko.

- Heat lamps and other fixtures can provide the tank with a basking area and a cooler area. You should ensure to turn on the heat lamp at day time, and turn it off at night time to create a 8 to 12 hours day/night cycle and not interrupt your pet gecko's sleeping pattern.

- You can also buy a reptile thermometer to easily help you in regulating temperatures and the cage's humidity levels.

Food, Supplements, Watering

- Crested geckos are omnivores. They feed off on gut – loaded/ live insects, veggies, and fruits.

- You need to also provide powder supplements for your crested gecko, this is equivalent to vitamins for us humans to protect them against diseases and strengthen the body.

Chapter Three: Crested Geckos as Pets

- You may need to install a watering system for your pet. You can use a spray bottle or dripper (w/c is much cheaper) or you can opt to buy an automatic misting system but it's much more expensive.

- Crested geckos usually drink the droplets of water upon misting. Therefore it must 100% chlorine free. (More on this in the nutrition chapter).

Water Bowls, Hide House, Substrate

- The water bowl should be large enough for your crested gecko to soak in. It should be placed on the opposite side of the cage.

- The hide house should be placed right over where the heat pads are located, and the under the heat lamp above the enclosure.

- The substrate should be preferably made out of loose coconut fiber. This is the ideal substrate for crested geckos as it will hold humidity inside the enclosure, which is also perfect for plants. It's best to keep it damp, but not watery.

Chapter Three: Crested Geckos as Pets

Veterinarian Consultations

- Be sure to save up for its medical needs and vet costs as crested geckos can get sick from time to time especially if you won't practice proper husbandry.

- You may also need to do some medical checkups and/or lab tests once in a while for your pet.

Branches and Plants/ Cage Decorations

- Crested geckos loves to climb on plants and trees, you should also purchase cage decors such as branches, leaves, live plants and other accessories to ensure that they'll live in a familiar habitat.

- You also need to buy a laying bin if in case you'd be breeding a crested gecko. The bin for female cresties can be quite expensive.

- You may also want to buy other cage decorations for your enclosure but make sure to not over - decorate it.

Chapter Three: Crested Geckos as Pets

Expenses Overview

- Crested Gecko breed: $35 - $100
- Glass Enclosure with a screen top or lid: average of $89 - $100 (depending on size/ accessories included)
- Glass Enclosure (complete set with regulators/heaters): $200 - $300
- Bedding or Substrate: $6/bag
- Water Dish(for adults/large): $20
- Heaters/Misting Equipment: $50 and up
- Basking Lamp/UVB bulbs: $100 more or less
- Heat and Water Temperature Regulator/ Gauges: $5 and up
- Hiding Spots: $5
- Laying bin: $10 - $15
- Food: These are the sample prices of commercial food for crested geckos. A meal with a more varied diet will be much pricey but more complete and has some added nutrients, here is a sample price for ordinary commercial food versus one with added nutrients:
    - Repashy Superfood Crested Meal Replacement Brand: $8.99 (3 oz)
    - Pangea Fruit Mix With Insects Crested Gecko Complete Diet: $19.99 (1/2 pounds)

Chapter Three: Crested Geckos as Pets

Pros and Cons of Keeping Crested Geckos

Here are some things you might want to ponder on before you acquire a crested gecko. Sure these pets are small, cute, and easy to maintain and keep but like any other pet species; they can still possess some disadvantages. Here are some of the pros and cons of owning a crested gecko, check them out and see if this is something that suits your personality or your expectations.

Pros

- **Does not need too much attention.** Crested geckos don't need to interact constantly with their owners. They can happily live and be satisfied in their enclosure as long as needs are properly met.
- **Adaptability.** Crested geckos has the ability to easily adapt to its environment
- **No exercise needed.** They get their 'exercise' and fun through climbing branches and hiding in plants or simply interacting with their own kind.
- **Small and easy to handle.** Doesn't take up too much space, and handling is not necessary.
- **Have no special needs.** Crested geckos compared to popular or high – energy pets are easy to keep since it doesn't demands attention.

Chapter Three: Crested Geckos as Pets

Cons

- Has quite a long lifespan (10 – 15 years)
- May come across as boring or non – interactive
- Cannot be handled or petted all the time
- May not be advisable for first time owners or young children

Chapter Three: Crested Geckos as Pets

Chapter Four: Acquiring Crested Geckos

Since crested geckos are exotic animal species, it's quite possible that you won't be able to find any kind of breed or the color you prefer in your local pet store. You might need to acquire it from a private breeder or a reptile hobbyist, or it may only be available in pet stores that offer all sorts of animals and not just the common household pets. Nevertheless, you can surely acquire a crested gecko as long as you know where to look and what kind of breeder to look for. This chapter will cover the common places where you can purchase crested geckos, and the traits of a reputable breeder and a healthy breed to ensure that you'll get nothing but the best quality crested gecko.

Chapter Four: Acquiring Crested Geckos

Tips When Acquiring a Crested Gecko

It is highly recommended that you only purchase a captive - bred crested gecko. Sure it may cost you a little extra dollars but it is worth it because you can be guaranteed that the crested gecko is healthy and doesn't have any illnesses or transmitted diseases. Aside from that it will also benefit captive breeding programs, and will help them to further breed healthy species in the future.

Avoid buying from backyard breeders. As much as possible, don't acquire a crested gecko from backyard breeders just because it's cheap. You may not be certain about its health, and the crested geckos they have may also just be caught in the wild and not bred in captivity. You may risk from the issues of importation damages. It happens when species are illegally imported/ caught in the wild.

It's also not recommended that you buy from pet stores. Local pet stores more often than not only sell crested geckos for profit, and the creatures are usually in poor condition because of improper husbandry, and unsanitary housing facility. On top of that, the needs of crested geckos are overlooked by pet stores.

You may opt for adoption. Try if you can find a crested gecko in a reptile adoption centers. The only downside is

Chapter Four: Acquiring Crested Geckos

you won't be guaranteed of its health/background but you can save the lives of this species.

Make sure that the species you're getting is the right breed of gecko. Before purchasing you should also first identify if the crested gecko is a captive breed or caught in the wild. It's important that you verify with the seller or provider the kind of crested gecko you are purchasing. If your provider is unsure then you may ask a reputable source or an expert in reptiles to identify the kind of breed/ color pattern you want to buy.

Purchase from legitimate breeders, crested gecko hobbyists, or during reptile conventions. These are some of the places where you can find passionate breeders who are also experts when it comes to all things gecko! You can also get referrals on where you can purchase a healthy crested gecko from several forums online or online communities. These communities usually have contacts, has history information regarding responsible breeding, and you can also get ideas on how to properly care for your new pet. Still be wary though and ensure that you're getting exactly what you pay for. Be wary of breeders or hobbyists who are selling crested geckos that are too young as well.

As much as possible, don't purchase very young crested geckos. Ensure that the species you're going to buy is already old and mature enough to be transferred. Hatchling

Chapter Four: Acquiring Crested Geckos

crested geckos are quite delicate and fragile because of their small size; you'll have more chance of successfully raising a much older crested gecko.

Quarantine your newly acquired pet. It's very ideal that you quarantine your crested gecko for at least more than a month before keeping them with other similar species. This is to ensure that your pet is healthy and is not a carrier of transmittable diseases. Doing a quarantine for exotic animals such as the crested gecko is important because these creatures don't show any signs of illnesses, and can even hold on to it for a long time without being noticed. Here are some steps you need to take for a successful quarantine period:

Step #1: Put your new crested gecko in a separate room, away from your other pets for at least 45 days.

Step #2: Make sure to feed and handle all your other pets before introducing or placing the newly quarantine gecko with them to avoid contamination.

Step #3: Make sure to use separate equipment for the quarantined gecko, and always wash your hands after handling them. Cage hygiene should always be done to prevent the spread of germs or parasites.

Chapter Four: Acquiring Crested Geckos

Step #4: You can also test your new pet's fecal sample at your vet for diagnosis and testing to ensure that they aren't suffering from any internal diseases/ disorders.

Step #5: After careful observation, and health testing, you can now introduce your crested gecko to its new home or other similar species. Do the same thing if you're planning to acquire more than 2 or 3 animals.

Is it legal to Keep Crested Geckos?

Crested geckos are not considered as endangered animals anymore. As mentioned earlier, they almost became extinct back in 1994, but thanks to the passionate breeders and hobbyists, they kept reproducing and improving the species. Here are some things you need to know regarding the legalities of owning one. Make sure to check with your local state to ensure that you're abiding the regulations regarding exotic animal keeping.

CITES Laws for Crested Geckos

The Convention on International Trade in Endangered Species (CITES) for wild fauna and flora are the governing body that is responsible in taking care of all animal species especially the endangered ones. Almost all countries in major continents all over the world are a

Chapter Four: Acquiring Crested Geckos

member of CITES including USA, Europe, Latin America, Asia and Australia. It is highly recommended that you have legal or proper documents regarding any animal or species you keep as pets to save you in case of any trouble. CITES has 3 appendices, and each appendix contains a list of different species in different categories, and therefore has different rules when it comes to keeping, exporting and trading. Most gecko species fall under the CITES II appendix. CITES II includes species that can be traded freely but cannot be taken from the wild.

Keeping Pet Ownership Documents

Keeping ownership documents can be essential especially if you're planning to travel with your pet. You just need to simply provide a document stating the name, identity of the species or your crested gecko as well as the name address, contact details and signature of the previous owner or where you bought it from. You may need to also provide your own personal details and signature. This document needs to be kept for future reference.

Chapter Four: Acquiring Crested Geckos

Conservation Issues/ Concerns

- All the gecko species including the crested gecko are all protected under international laws and these laws should be abide to ensure the stability of the species' population.

- Crested gecko breeders and pet owners believe that it is an owner's responsibility to take care of these exotic animals and preserve its species.

- Illegal pet trading is a big problem because it has a huge impact in conservation issues.

- If you don't have the time, expertise, and money to take care of these endangered creatures, it may be better to turn them over to experts or wildlife authorities.

- The crested geckos you will catch in the wild or near your area needs to be raised properly.

- For first time keepers, it's highly recommended that you purchase one that is bred in captivity or those who are newly hatched.

Chapter Four: Acquiring Crested Geckos

Tips When Choosing a Reputable Breeder

Selecting a reputable breeder can be hard especially if you're a first time reptile keeper. It's highly recommended that before acquiring a crested gecko or any reptile species for this matter that you first ask someone who's already knowledgeable on how to buy one. If there's no one available at the moment, your best bet is to do as much research as you can about your prospective breeder, and get many referrals from other customers that have previously transacted with your chosen breeder. Here are some more tips to keep in mind:

Good breeders must be knowledgeable about the breeds. They should be able to give you specific information about the breed. Do take note that the primary reason for breeding should be because it is their hobby or passion, and not just for appearance or selling purposes.

Breeders tend to know a lot about the species they breed so they must supply more specific information that you can't easily get online. If they only tell you general information, chances are they're not really interested with their pets. They should be able to teach you how to properly set up the enclosure, where to place it, and the right temperature/humidity levels needed.

Chapter Four: Acquiring Crested Geckos

Legit breeders know how to establish a good relationship with their potential/existing buyers. Be sure to ask for referrals from their previous buyers so that you can ask them about the pet they've bought from this breeder, and if they have good rapport.

See how interested or proud the breeder is. You can easily spot an enthusiastic gecko breeder if all they want is to talk to you about how they raise their breeds. They will not hesitate to answer your questions and at the same time ask questions of their own. They are also proud of their collections.

Ensure that the breeder is someone who is approachable, and are open for mentorship. If you think they'll be hard tp reach during the buying or inquiry process, chances are that they will be unresponsive to you after the sale.

A reputable breeder will walk you through every step of the process. They are also happy to say 'no' to you or to any potential clients on whom they think won't be good keepers of their pets, that's how much they care. In order to find that out, you can ask them what their criteria is when finding a responsible keeper.

Chapter Four: Acquiring Crested Geckos

Know what to ask. Here are some questions you can ask your potential breeders; information about crested gecko or this particular color/pattern; the things needed for its enclosure; stores or brands of supplies/ food for the crested gecko; the right size or material use for the enclosure; how the crested gecko were bred and raised; how often to feed it and the proper nutrition; how to set up the right temperature for its habitat; how many years has the breeder been raising crested geckos, and if there are any warranties or health certificates.

List of Breeders and Rescue Websites

Here is the list of breeders and websites that sell crested geckos:

Breeders and Rescue Websites

Morph Market
<https://www.morphmarket.com/us/c/reptiles/lizards/crested-geckos/home >

The Urban Gecko
<http://www.theurbangecko.com/sale>

Chapter Four: Acquiring Crested Geckos

Moon Valley Reptiles
<http://www.moonvalleyreptiles.com/store/crested-geckos >

Epic Geckos
<http://www.epicgeckos.com/available >

Gecko Spot
<http://www.geckospot.com>

Underground Reptiles
<https://undergroundreptiles.com/product-category/animals/geckos/>

CB Reptile
<https://www.cbreptile.com>

Back Water Reptiles
<http://www.backwaterreptiles.com/geckos/crested-gecko-for-sale.html>

AC Reptiles
<http://acreptiles.com/new_store/index.php?dispatch=categories.view&category_id=1>

Crested Gecko
<http://www.crestedgecko.com/geckos-for-sale/byhierarchy/18/1944 >

Chapter Four: Acquiring Crested Geckos

Pets 4 Homes UK

<https://www.pets4homes.co.uk/sale/reptiles/gecko/>

Exotic – Pets UK

<https://www.exotic-pets.co.uk/geckos-for-sale.html>

Petco.com

<https://www.petco.com/shop/en/petcostore/product/crested-gecko-5004154--1>

Pet Smart

<https://www.petsmart.com/reptile/live-reptiles/snakes-turtles-and-more/eyelash-crested-gecko-4151185.html>

Pets at Home

<http://www.petsathome.com/shop/en/pets/crested-gecko>

Reptile Rapture

<http://reptilerapture.net/geckos.html>

Lilly Exotics

<http://www.lillyexotics.co.uk>

Tortoise Town

<https://www.tortoisetown.com/crested-geckos-for-sale/>

Chapter Four: Acquiring Crested Geckos

Tips When Choosing a Crested Gecko

- **Check its health.** If you are a first time crested gecko or gecko owner, it is best to start off with a healthy one because an ill pet can be very challenging to the inexperienced, this is particularly for those who have acquired the pet from an adoption center.

- **Notice any sort of illness or ill behavior.** Crested geckos are the kind of animals that do not show any signs of diseases for a long time without being noticed. It's imperative that before purchasing one you should look for basic signs of a healthy gecko (which we will discuss in the next section).

- **Have a checklist of your health standard.** Once you have already determined a certain reputable breeder, your next step is to actually pick out the crested gecko you want. Ensure that the crested geckos they have available are healthy and ready to go home with you.

Chapter Four: Acquiring Crested Geckos

Signs of Healthy Crested Geckos

Sign #1: Active and arboreal. A healthy crested gecko should be active in its environment and since it's an arboreal animal, you might want to observe them climbing up and down the branches inside their enclosure.

Sign #2: Balance and without any mobility disorders. The crested gecko should be able to move about the enclosure with good balance without falling or stumbling. As what we've discussed regarding their foot pads, the crested geckos should be able to climb branches without falling or slipping out.

Sign #3: Eyelash and fringe eyes. The eyes should be full, open at all times and actively looking all around. They wouldn't be called 'eyelash geckos' for no reason.

Sign #4: Strong limbs. The arm and leg bones should all be straight, toes should all be intact and the crested geckos should have a strong grip.

Sign #5: Healthy skin and vibrant color. Obviously their skin should have 'crests' on it or a spiny – looking structure. The color should be solid, and if there's any pattern, it should be present throughout the back, the head or neck area, and in its limbs.

Subject for Second Thoughts!

If the crested gecko exhibits these signs, you might want to have second thoughts about it, and re – consider:

Sign #1: Inactive. You don't want to acquire a lethargic crested gecko. If it is lying on the bottom of the cage, and not climbing up and down as often as it should be, chances are that the gecko is sick.

Sign #2: Eye problems. It exhibits sunken or swollen eyes.

Sign #3: Swollen limbs promoting mobility issues. Legs that are bent, curved, appear to have multiple joints or have swellings at the joints.

Sign #4: Uneven and unhealthy skin. Wrinkly, crusty or dry skin, bumps, cuts or bruises, or patches of abnormal colored skin is a no – no!

Sign #5: Other obvious health issues. Blood at the mouth; swollen jaw; breathing problems; genetic problems; behavioral problems.

Chapter Four: Acquiring Crested Geckos

Chapter Five: Housing Needs of Crested Geckos

Now that you've acquired your new pet gecko, it's time to prepare its new home right in your own home! Changing homes or environment can be quite a shock for most pets. It can cause them to be stressed out especially if the enclosure or habitat is not like what they were raised in. This is why providing them with adequate habitat that is quite similar to their previous habitat while they're still in the care of their breeders is important. This chapter will cover all the things you need to know about preparing a new living environment for your pet crested gecko. Just give them some time to adjust to it, and be patient.

Chapter Five: Housing Needs of Crested Geckos

Acclimating New Crested Geckos

It may definitely take some time for your new crested geckos to adjust to its new environment. These creatures can get stressed especially if they were shipped or transferred to a strange surrounding. If this happens, you can expect them to not eat food for a couple of days to a few weeks – and that's okay. Just make sure that the enclosure is clean, the temperature is right, and still offer nutritious foods every now and then, until they settle in their new home. This may definitely take a while, so keep an eye out and take the time to observe them.

One of the factors that can cause further stress to your new reptile pet is the enclosure. Most of these crested geckos were raised by breeders in plastic boxes in a sort of rack system. Usually baby crested geckos got used to a type of environment where there's no overhead lighting and their basking spot comes from a heat source attached under the box. All of a sudden, these creatures will be transferred to its new owner where most of the time the type of enclosure is a glass tank. There's nothing wrong with placing your pets in a glass tank, the only problem is that species like crested geckos don't like 'change.' Much like humans, the unfamiliar scares them.

Chapter Five: Housing Needs of Crested Geckos

Here are some ways on how you can acclimate your new pet to its new enclosure:

- Ensure that the light bulb you're using is either a red/blue bulb with low light emissions. One example is a nocturnal reptile bulb.

- When it comes to the heat source, you can use heat pads to provide a sort of belly heat for your crested geckos.

- Ensure that the hiding place inside the enclosure is dark/ covered, warm, and just enough for their size to make them feel secure.

- You can handle them in the first 2 weeks but not too much; just enough to let them know your presence or get them used to your scent.

- You can cover the 4 sides of the glass with a black background like a cardboard, and remove one side every week so that they can adjust to the new enclosure. After about a month you can remove the 4 black cardboard.

- When it comes to feeding, as much as possible try feeding the same food that it was consuming at its

Chapter Five: Housing Needs of Crested Geckos

breeder as dietary change can be quite stressful for them.

- Before adding another crested gecko in your collection, take time to quarantine it by putting the new creature in a separate enclosure for at least 30 – 45 days. If you plan in housing your crested geckos in one enclosure, ensure that they are also the same size or the same species.

- Try not to place more than one male crested gecko in an enclosure even if the cage is big. It will stress out the female geckos.

Habitat Requirements

Reptiles such as crested geckos are cold – blooded (ectothermic). This means that these creatures adapt to the temperature of the environment they are in so that they can regulate their own body temperature. This is the reason why creating the right temperature levels for them is important. The enclosure of all cold – blooded animals should have a cool and warm area (for basking). This kind of environment will cater to their warm/ cool temperature needs.

Chapter Five: Housing Needs of Crested Geckos

And since crested geckos are arboreal animals, you can expect them to climb on plants and trees which is why you should make sure that the branches, leaves and/ or live plants you're going to buy are fresh and also not poisonous. Cut any pointy twigs to avoid your geckos in getting scratch or cuts. When it comes to the water bowls, it should be large enough for your crested gecko to soak in, and ideally it should be placed on the opposite side of the cage. Make sure to replace the water daily to avoid being contaminated. The water should also be clean and chlorine free because this is where they'll take a bath and drink as well.

Enclosure Size

The tank should preferably be 29 – gallon, and made out of solid glass. This is enough for 3 crested gecko adults. You can opt for a high tank with a size of about 20 gallon but it can be quite large especially for a juvenile crested geckos.

The enclosure should be secured so that your crested gecko won't be able to escape. Ensure that you have a metal mesh on top of the cage. It should be made out of metal because you also want the light from the heat lamp benefit your crested gecko since it's usually place on top of the enclosure (for basking).

Chapter Five: Housing Needs of Crested Geckos

It's also advisable that you provide a hide house for your pet gecko. Ideally, it should be placed right over where the heat pads are located, and the under the heat lamp above the enclosure. When it comes to the substrate, it should be preferably made out of loose coconut fiber. This is the ideal substrate for crested geckos as it will hold humidity inside the enclosure, which is also perfect for plants.

Heating and Lighting

Adequate lighting like a 75 watt bulb heat, and under tank heaters or heat pads underneath will provide appropriate temperature and humidity levels inside your pet gecko's cage enclosure. It's important to note that your crested gecko won't be spending too much time at the bottom of the cage.

You may also need to purchase things like a UVB bulb though it's not really required as some reptiles can benefit from low levels of UVB light including the crested gecko.

However, your crested gecko still might need Vitamin D since they wouldn't be exposed to the sun compared to if they were staying outside. You can turn on the UVB light for about 8 to 12 hours. That way they can get it along during their basking time. When it comes to heat lamps and other

Chapter Five: Housing Needs of Crested Geckos

fixtures you can provide the tank with a basking area and a cooler area. You should ensure to turn on the heat lamp at day time, and turn it off at night time to create eight to twelve hours day/night cycle and not interrupt your pet gecko's sleeping pattern. It's very important that the heat lamps, UVB lights, and other heat source fixtures are out of reach of your pet crested gecko otherwise thermal burns can be fatal for them.

Required Temperature

The temperature should always be regulated and monitored daily. Your reptile thermometer is essential when checking temperatures and ensuring that the places in the enclosure is just the right condition. An important note though, if ever the room temperature is below 70 degrees especially at night time, what you can do is provide a supplemental infrared light or a ceramic heat fixture. Don't worry though because such lighting fixtures will not blind out your pet crested gecko while it's sleeping but it will provide the heat necessary. If the temperature is not right, your crested gecko will most likely become ill or have respiratory issues and lose appetite as they'll have a hard time digesting their food if they the heat they are receiving is not adequate. The humidity levels should be kept at 80%.

Chapter Five: Housing Needs of Crested Geckos

Housing Needs Checklist

- 29 – Gallon glass tank or vivarium that can suit 1 to 3 adult crested geckos
- Metal mesh on top (for security)
- Under Tank Heater or heat pads (should be place on the same side of the basking light)
- Hide house (place more than one if you have a few collections living in the same enclosure)
- Water bowl (big enough for your crested gecko/s)
- Heat bulbs
- Reptile Thermometer or humidity gauge (don't stick it inside the tank)
- Substrate (preferably coconut fiber)
- UVB bulb

Reminders When Cleaning the Enclosure

- Spot cleaning is very important because it means that you thoroughly clean not just the cage of your pet gecko but also all the materials you placed inside the cage. You need to clean your pet's habitat enclosure regularly as well.

- As mentioned earlier, the humidity within the enclosure can be a perfect breeding ground for the growth of bacteria. Most reptiles can be prone to skin

Chapter Five: Housing Needs of Crested Geckos

and bacterial infection if left alone in unclean surroundings for long which is why regular cage maintenance and cleaning should be part of your routine.

- Regular cleaning prevents the possible transmission of diseases which can be found in the fecal matter of reptiles, and which may be transmissible to humans. Not only will this keep the interior of the enclosure clean, odor-free, and healthy, but it will also keep you and your family safe and healthy.

- Spot cleaning the interior of the cage should be done as often as possible – at least once a day or once every other day. When you spot clean your pet's enclosure, you should make sure that any fecal matter is removed, the shedded skin is removed as well as the uneaten or left over food. The water bowls should also be replaced more than once a week to prevent bacterial growth.

- During the cleaning process, you will need to relocate the gecko so that you can clean and sterilize the entire tank components such as its hiding spots, substrate, plants/branches etc.

- You may need to temporarily relocate your crested gecko to a different tank. As usual, make sure that

Chapter Five: Housing Needs of Crested Geckos

this cage is secure and clean, and is sufficiently ventilated.

- Before doing a full cleanse of your pet's tank, you must first find a suitable temporary cage for your crested gecko.

Chapter Six: Nutrition for Your Crested Gecko

This chapter will cover all the things you need when feeding a nutritious and balance diet for your pet cresty. Feeding your pet with the right food and a varied diet will contribute in their good health; vibrant color, strong physique, and can also make them strong against diseases. If your pet cresty is satisfied and happy with the food they are eating, they'll grow quickly, they'll be active, and they'll be

Chapter Six: Nutrition for Your Crested Gecko

happy staying with you. You have to keep in mind that food is the major source of strength for these kinds of creatures. What you want to do is to feed them the diet that they usually eat in the wild but this time, it's much more enticing, much more delicious and nutritious and also quite easy to grab – thanks to you!

Commercial Gecko Diet (CGD)

One of the most popular crested gecko diets has to be the meal replacement powder which is the Repashy and Pangea food brand. Most keepers use the Repashy Crested Gecko diet; this is a really simple diet mix and a lot of people also use it. The Pangea brand on the other hand is an expert in developing a varied diet for your crested gecko.

These commercial crested gecko diets are widely available in your local pet stores and big brand supermarkets. It is a powdered meal supplement that should be mixed with water to form a sort of paste that your crested gecko can easily digest. You can feed your crested gecko with the commercial diet daily or every other day. These brands contain nutritious diet that goes along with a good balance of supplements that your pet needs.

When feeding them with such, what you can do after thoroughly mixing it with water is to place it in a small food

Chapter Six: Nutrition for Your Crested Gecko

dish at night so they can feed on it, and remove the uneaten food in the morning.

Fruits and Live Prey

Some crested geckos refuse the Repashy and Pangea brands or other similar meal replacement powder. You can go for things like insects such as gut - loaded crickets and locusts. Most keepers actually just feed their crested geckos with organic diet like live insects which is probably the reason why some species might not like the ready to eat food brands - which is perfectly fine as long as it is balance and you offer something of a varied and nutritious diet.

Crested geckos are omnivores which mean they both feed on live prey and organic food like fruits. They also feed on nectars which is part of their natural diet in the wild. Feeding your pet gecko with organic and live diet is very beneficial because it gives these creatures an opportunity to hunt for their food just like what they do in the wild. Crickets are very jumpy and moves rapidly which is perfect because it gives your crested gecko some form of exercise through hunting their prey.

Another thing you can feed your crested gecko as a treat is fruits such as mango, bananas, peach, papaya,

Chapter Six: Nutrition for Your Crested Gecko

apricots, fig, pear, strawberries, grapes and the likes. If you are interested in feeding your crested gecko with fruit, it's important to note that you should not feed them citrus fruits like oranges and lemons because for some reason it's bad for these animals.

When feeding fruits what you can do is to mashed it up or cut it into little pieces so that your crested gecko can easily consume it. As much as possible, never feed your crested gecko with baby food because it contains too much sugar which can be bad for your reptile pet. You can alternate feeding your pet with fruits, live prey, and also a commercial food.

Protein and Supplements

The protein source of crested geckos comes from gut – loading their foods. Gut – loading means dusting the live prey with supplement powder so that when they eat it, it'll be nutritious. Never feed your pet with wild caught insects as it can carry diseases and be passed on to your pet or make them ill. All live prey should be gut – loaded at least 24 hours before feeding it to your gecko. The supplements you're going to feed to your crickets/ locusts/ meal worms or other insects must have a good balance of vitamins and minerals that are targeted to meet your crested gecko's

Chapter Six: Nutrition for Your Crested Gecko

needs. It should also contain calcium and Vitamin D3, and must be of great quality.

Water

As mentioned in previous chapters, you should be able to provide your pet crested gecko with fresh, 100% chlorine – free and clean water. You should place the water bowl in the cool area of the enclosure, and you must change it every day or as needed. Your cresty will most likely drink from the misted drops of water inside the enclosure, so ensure that you spray or mist the cage at least twice in a day. Using tap water is not recommended as it may contain some chlorine or heavy metals. Sometimes the water filters may not remove unwanted chemicals, which is why unflavored bottle water or bottle natural spring water is ideal. If you're going to use tap water, it's best that you de – chlorinate it using treatments that are available in pet stores. You should also avoid using distilled water because even if it's clean, it also lacks minerals which are essential for your pet, and because of this, it may cause medical problems. Whenever you're misting, make sure that you don't allow their cage to become too damp.

Chapter Six: Nutrition for Your Crested Gecko

Feeding Tips for Your Crested Gecko

- The staple insect to feed your cresty should be crickets. The crickets' size should be no larger than the space between your pet's eyes.

- Make sure to gut – load the prey or other insects you're going to feed your crested gecko so that the nutrients will also be passed on to your pet once they consume it.

- It's not necessary to gutload the insects with calcium and Vitamin D3 if you're already feeding your pet gecko with a commercial meal supplement or crested gecko diet since most brands already included Vitamin D3 in the mixture. Too much D3 might have adverse effects.

- You can feed your crested gecko with at least 4 to 6 gut - loaded insect, and feed it to them 2 to 3 times per week.

Chapter Six: Nutrition for Your Crested Gecko

- When feeding your crested gecko, you can try and toss the food to them one at a time, and see if they are interested in consuming more.

- Aside from feeding insects, fruits, and commercial meal supplements (CGD), you can also mix in a couple of waxworms or butterworms to create variety. You can offer 2 to 3 small worms for your crested gecko and see if he likes it.

- You must remember to remove all the uneaten foods/insects in the cage especially if it's a live prey because it can harm your crested gecko.

- You can also transfer your cresty to a separate empty enclosure whenever you're doing the feeding. Most keepers do this to ensure that the crested gecko can eat all their food, and make hunting easier for them.

Chapter Six: Nutrition for Your Crested Gecko

Chapter Seven: Dealing with Your Crested Geckos

This chapter will cover more about the behavior of your crested gecko when handling them and during their shedding period. Proper handling is essential especially for this small creatures because if not you can risk them falling off because it can potentially break their tails off and can also injure them badly. Taking proper precautions when handling them can be life – saving. Learning how to deal with their behavior and taking the time to observe them on how they respond to things like handling, feeding, shedding, and co – existing with other crested geckos will give you a better insight and understanding.

Chapter Seven: Dealing with Your Crested Geckos

Crested Gecko Behavior and Interaction

Crested geckos are gentle and sweet little reptiles that can be easily tamed and handle even for first – time gecko keepers. However, crested geckos can tend to be a bit jumpy at first so it's better to handle them properly. Try to restrict from touching them too much especially if they have just been transferred to their new enclosure to avoid stressing them out. You can pick them up at least twice a week just so they can get used to your scent. And since crested geckos usually have vibrant colors and patterns, you can expect them to camouflage among the branches and leaves inside their enclosure.

Whenever you're handling them, make sure that you support their limbs and not let them drop their tails because their tails don't regenerate if ever it was cut loose.

How to Handle Your Crested Gecko

Most crested geckos tolerate regular handling (after a few weeks adjusting to their new environment). Once they already got the 'feels' of their new cage, they can be pretty calm when a human touch them or handle them. They don't

Chapter Seven: Dealing with Your Crested Geckos

particularly bite but if ever a cresty nips out on you, don't worry because it won't be that painful.

It's also important to note that even if your cresties are docile and can be left in their own devises, they still need to be monitored from time to time just to ensure that they don't accidentally hurt themselves or escape from their enclosure. Crested geckos are arboreal creatures which is why they are prone to falling off. A fall from about 1 foot high or more can definitely injure them and even kill them which is why whenever you're handling them, you need to be very careful because they like to jump a lot, make sure that they will jump to you or to a soft surface to avoid accidents.

When handling, you can let them jump from your hand to your other hand; let them hop freely and move your hand (or next obstacle) so they can easily target their next move. This can also serve as a form of exercise for them. Don't restrain or squeeze the crested gecko too hard because you can easily cut their tail off, and even stress them out.

Crested geckos are not advisable to young children especially the naughty ones because they can easily let the crested geckos hit the ground or squeeze them. Make sure to supervise your children if you let them handle your crested geckos.

Chapter Seven: Dealing with Your Crested Geckos

Another important thing to note when handling crested geckos is to make sure that your hands are clean before and after you handle them. Proper hygiene is important for you and your pet. This is because most reptiles carry salmonella bacteria which don't really affect your pet's health, but it can give you gastrointestinal illness if you don't wash your hands after handling them. It can cause serious risk to young children and also compromise one's immune system.

Make sure to wash your hands with soap after handling them, clean their enclosure as needed, and ensure that the cleaning materials like the soap you'll use when cleaning their bowls or cage are also reptile friendly.

Crested Gecko Shedding

Crested geckos will tend to shed their skin from time to time. They usually shed in patches like most reptiles. Don't be surprised if ever your crested gecko has periods where its color becomes dull as it may mean that they're preparing to shed off their skin. Never ever peel off your pet's skin if ever it doesn't come off naturally as it can be painful for your little reptile.

Chapter Seven: Dealing with Your Crested Geckos

Reptiles living in the wild deal with their shedding much easier because the environment is generally humid, and they have unlimited access to bodies of water where they can soak at their own will. Shedding is essential because this is a reptile's way of getting rid of the old skin and replaces it with a new layer of skin. What usually happens is that the new skin begins to separate from the old. Now if your pet's cage is too dry because you don't mist it, your crested gecko may have a hard time when shedding.

Go to your vet if ever your pet didn't properly shed its skin off. You might also want to create more humidity in the enclosure by spraying or misting it twice a day whenever your crested gecko entered its shedding period. However, ensure that the spray or droplets of water is completely dried off before you turn off the light at night because if not it may contribute to respiratory illnesses.

Chapter Seven: Dealing with Your Crested Geckos

Chapter Eight: Breeding Your Crested Geckos

One of the coolest things when it comes to owning reptile species such as the crested geckos is having the opportunity to breed them. Keepers and first – time owners of crested geckos eventually progress to becoming breeders themselves. Of course, breeding may not be for everyone, and it's also not necessary if you don't want to breed your pet gecko. When it comes to breeding, different species will need different requirements for it to become successful, and to also ensure that the offspring is healthy, and your pet gecko's health won't also be compromised.

Chapter Eight: Breeding Your Crested Geckos

This chapter will cover everything you need to know about the basics of breeding crested geckos; the dos and don'ts; and also the requirements needed.

Sexual Maturity and Sexual Dimorphism

For females, most breeders recommend that you wait for your pet cresties to reach a certain weight; at least 40 to 50 grams for females, and minimum of 35 grams and above for males. Male crested geckos may tend to be generally smaller than the opposite sex but as long as they reach maturity, and the ideal weight there'll be no problem with their sizes.

When it comes to identifying a male from a female, male crested geckos usually have a bulge in their tails while females don't develop such bulge. The bulge on their tails are perhaps the only obvious sign you can look out for if you want to identify their sex but other than that crested geckos are not sexually dimorphic creatures unlike other reptiles where there are many physical characteristics that can be used as reference to easily identify a male from a female.

Chapter Eight: Breeding Your Crested Geckos

Breeding Requirements

When it comes to the size of the enclosure, you may opt to buy an 18 x 18 x 18 cage for breeding pairs. If you plan on breeding 1 male cresty to 4 female crested geckos, you may need a slightly larger enclosure that measures about 18 x 18 x 24.

Whenever you're setting up your breeding cage, you want to make sure that you have a functional use of the space. The last thing you want is to buy a cage that is too large for nothing. It's ideal that you maximize the cage with a substantial amount of cage decors such as branches, leaves or live plants, hide house, and substrate as well as other needed requirements. You should also keep in mind that the enclosure should be adequate enough to make your breeding crested geckos comfortable and also allow them to have a space where they can do the mating, and laying of eggs. You want to only provide something that is enough to create a sort of natural barrier so that they won't stress each other too much. If your crested gecko feel pressured or feels like it is forced to breed with another species, they may tend to run – away.

The best soil or substrate you can provide your breeding cresties to use in the lay box is either of the following:

Chapter Eight: Breeding Your Crested Geckos

- Eco Earth
- Coconut Fiber
- Peat Moss

These substrates can hold the humidity inside the enclosure very well. If you have a substrate that dries up quickly, it may run the risk of the eggs drying up easily which means you can lose it. Make sure that when you get a substrate you mix it with a bit of water to have that moist effect and not to the point where the water will be dripping off of it. The substrate should be able to hold the moisture in for a couple of weeks.

Once you filled the lay box with substrate, you can just cut one hole in it where your female crested gecko can crawl in and also lay their eggs.

When it comes to requirements for incubation, you can let the eggs hatch in a container about the size of a shoe box with about an inch of soil / substrate. You want to bury the eggs halfway in the soil.

Feeding Your Breeding Cresties

There'll be times that some crested geckos will be more territorial than others, which is why when it comes to feeding you may want to prepare 2 to 3 feeding bowls so

Chapter Eight: Breeding Your Crested Geckos

that you can also maximize the space inside the enclosure and avoid territoriality among breeding geckos especially breeding groups. If you also find your crested geckos having issues getting along with each other, perhaps providing more food bowls will help solve this problem. This is because breeding can be quite rough especially for pet geckos that never had an experience being bred before. This could get them to become quite aggressive at times towards the opposite sex.

Breeding Basics

The breeding process in captivity is of course very different to the way they do it in the wild. In captivity, there are many factors involve like your breeding purposes, maximizing the eggs/ productivity and the conditions.

The breeding season for crested geckos generally depends on where you live and also the average room temperature. If you can set your house temperature to a constant (say around 75 degrees) that could work out as well. You can basically breed them all year round, and use the seasons in your state to your advantage so that you can maximize breeding of your pet cresties. For those living in states that are experiencing the 4 seasons, it's also ideal to pair them up in the last 3 weeks of the winter season because

Chapter Eight: Breeding Your Crested Geckos

in that way, the crested geckos won't be as aggressive or as active when it comes to breeding, and your pets will just ease in to the next seasons like spring to summer seasons. This is also a great way to ensure that both your male and female crested geckos are not beaten up too much during mating/ reproduction process. What you want to do is to give your female crested geckos at least 3 to 4 months rest after breeding it or after recently laying eggs so that they can recover from the whole process.

Once your crested gecko lay their eggs inside the lay box, you'll notice them staying inside it with their head buried under the substrate/ soil this is a sign that your pet will be laying eggs in the next few days/ weeks. Once they are ready to lay eggs, they'll just deposit it under the substrate and bury it.

Crested geckos will lay an average of 6 to 10 clutches (2 eggs per clutch) every month or so though it can vary. Another interesting breeding fact is that your female crested geckos can have 10 years of productivity which means they can produce offspring and get their eggs fertilized during this period. You can maximize it even more through feeding them with high quality and balance food. Calcium is very important when your crested gecko is breeding. You want to ensure that you feed them with gut – loaded or calcium dusted insects like crickets since breeding crested geckos

Chapter Eight: Breeding Your Crested Geckos

will need extra protein, fat, and calcium to keep producing good quality eggs and healthy offspring.

Incubation

Once your female cresty lay their eggs, you're going to see a reddish ring once you rotate the egg and put it under the light. If the entire egg already gives off a red color or a red shade under the flashlight that's a sign that there's an embryo in it and it's fertilized. Infertile eggs on the other hand are quite smaller; the shell is not as hard and when placed under the light it gives off a yellow color. If you don't see a red ring after thoroughly checking on it, you can still incubate the egg if you like or if you're not as sure.

There are various incubation methods you can try perlite, vermiculite or super hatch techniques. The easiest method is the super hatch. What you need to do is just soak the super hatch in water for about a few minutes, and then drain it so that the super hatch can retain the moisture needed. Once you drain it off, the super hatch usually change in color which tells you if the substrate is moist or not.

You should incubate the eggs from 70 to 84 degrees Fahrenheit. The longer you incubate them (say about 3

Chapter Eight: Breeding Your Crested Geckos

months), the more likely the baby crested gecko is larger and stronger. Do note that you don't need to keep adding water to the substrate once you already bury the eggs in it this is because if you put in too much water, you can sort of drown the eggs or the embryo inside it. Just leave it there, wait for it to hatch and restrict from touching it especially during the later stages of incubation to avoid any mishaps.

You may want to record the day the egg was laid, the incubation period, and the hatching day so that you can keep tab on the whole process. This is one of the most important things you need to do when breeding crested geckos. You need to document the breed pairs, the offspring, the laying period, how many clutches etc. so that you'll have a sort of history of the breed. This is also important especially if you plan on becoming a legit breeder; you need to know when your female cresty is most productive, you need to know if you already maximize its reproductive years already, and it will allow you to replicate the results (color/pattern breeding) or avoid a certain result (genetic defects, poor color) in the next breeding season.

Chapter Nine: Common Illnesses of Crested Geckos

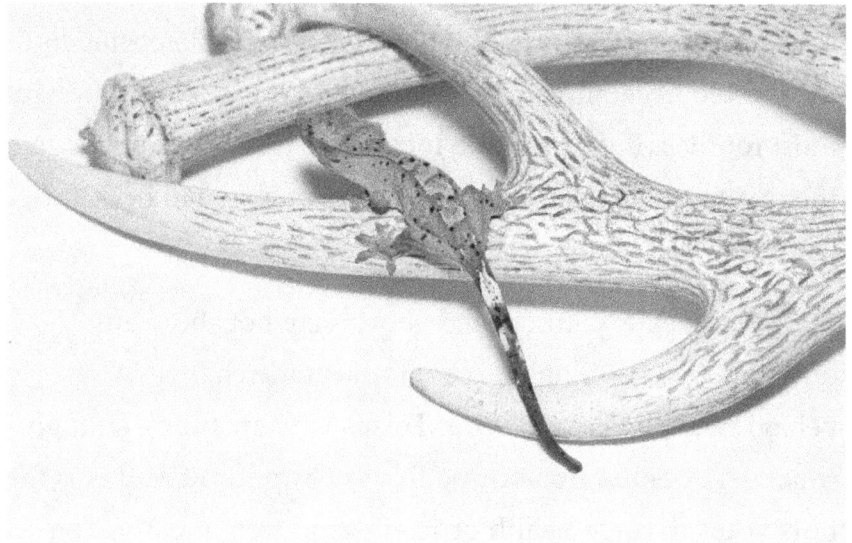

Your crested geckos may seem healthy most of the time but since these little creatures don't really show obvious signs you may not be able to notice that they're already suffering from some sort of illness. This is the reason why monitoring their health, providing them with nutritious diet, and practicing proper husbandry is essential because it can contribute to their health issues. Take the time to learn some of the most common crested gecko illnesses in this chapter so that you'll be aware of what to look out for and be able to do some adjustments here and there. You need to also ensure that you have a trusty exotic veterinarian that will help you in case your pet suffers such illnesses.

Chapter Nine: Common Illnesses of Crested Geckos

Common Health Problems

Crested geckos are generally healthy but they can still be exposed to various health issues. It's not just specific to the crested gecko breed species though, it is also common in most reptiles. If you want to make sure that your reptile gets the treatment he needs as quickly as possible you need to learn how to identify the symptoms of disease.

However your crested gecko may not show any outward signs of illness except for a subtle change in behavior or physical activity. This is why spending enough time and attention to your pet is very important as this is the how you can catch health problems and treat it early. The sooner you identify the symptoms, the sooner your vet can take action and the more likely your crested gecko will be able to make a full recovery.

This section will cover the common illnesses of crested geckos, its causes, symptoms, prevention tips, and possible treatment options as well. Feel free to consult your vet and ask about certain illnesses that could pose a threat to your crested gecko's health so that you'll be aware of how to prevent it.

Chapter Nine: Common Illnesses of Crested Geckos

Disease	Definition / Cause	Symptoms	Treatment/ Prevention
Impaction	This happens when your crested geckos especially the hatchlings eats some of the soil/ substrate causing it to become impacted in their guts.	The common signs of impaction are if your crested gecko starts to lose its appetite or appear lethargic. You'll never know if it's suffering from impaction or not unless they are diagnose.	If your pet seems lethargic or is slowly losing appetite, the best way is to bring it to the vet and get it treated.
Incomplete Skin Sloughing	This happens when the crested geckos' skins become too	Dry patches of skin	If your pet accumulated lots of skin, and it is stuck in them

Chapter Nine: Common Illnesses of Crested Geckos

	dried up.		what you need to do is place them in a damp moss or container with wet moss overnight in order to soften the skin. You can try and gently remove it once it comes off, but be very careful especially the dried skin around the eyes, and toes.

Chapter Nine: Common Illnesses of Crested Geckos

| Dehydration | Known as one of the leading health issues among crested geckos and other gecko breeds | Symptoms include sunken eyes (although it can also be caused by other health problems), orange urine, sunken head and sudden weight loss. | Make sure to maintain the appropriate humidity and also give your pet access to drippers because it can help in improving their hydration and make them frequent drinkers. You can also use showers as long as it is properly supervised or controlled, it can help simulate a |

Chapter Nine: Common Illnesses of Crested Geckos

rain.

If your gecko is always dehydrated it can lead to potential serious illnesses in the long run.

Make sure that your crested geckos have a follow - up check to the reptile vet if such symptoms don't improve.

Chapter Nine: Common Illnesses of Crested Geckos

Skin Burns	Skin burns happens when your pet are always near their basking light, or if the basking level is just too hot for them. Take note though that the skin doesn't actually have to touch the light for it to get burned.	Symptoms include blisters, patches and redness. The burned skin could also be peeled off. Usually there's a yellow discharge under the burned skin as well. The common spots for skin burns are the spine, casqued, and knees.	Always make sure that your basking light has the proper temperature to prevent skin burns. If you discover that your cresty has been suffering from burns, bring him to a vet immediately because bacterial infections or fungus can also happen if it is not immediately treated.

Chapter Nine: Common Illnesses of Crested Geckos

Floppy – Tail Syndrome	Crested geckos are very prone in experiencing floppy tail syndrome. It could be caused by lack of calcium or exercise.	Abnormal tail movement	To prevent this, you should ensure that your pet is getting the right nutrition, and doesn't lack any of it particularly calcium and Vitamin D3. You might also want to provide more arboreal cage décor to keep them moving and have an opportunity to exercise.
Metabolic Bone	This disease is caused by	Bent leg bones,	If prevented, the bones can

Chapter Nine: Common Illnesses of Crested Geckos

Disease (MBD)	a lack in dietary calcium, improper lighting, and also imbalanced nutrition.	double elbows, stunted growth, decrease in the use of its tongue, double knees, misaligned mouth, soft jaw	be treated with proper medications, and it can heal over time. Proper husbandry such as enough access to UVB lighting as well as proper nutrition can correct the calcium imbalance in the body
Fungal Dermatitis	This is also very common among crested geckos and	Common symptoms is ulcer, lethargy, appetite loss, and visible	Bring your pet to the vet as soon as you see such symptoms. You should

Crested Geckos as Pets

Chapter Nine: Common Illnesses of Crested Geckos

	reptiles in general	patches in the skin	also optimize its enclosure. Vets will usually treat it with topical medications.
Intestinal Parasites	Intestinal parasites are composed of microscopic worms and protozoa that basically lives inside your gecko's intestine; these kinds of parasites are very common among captive bred crested	The usual signs of intestinal parasites are smelly feces, lethargy, weight loss and lack of appetite as well as vomiting.	The treatment involves deworming medications though it still depends on the kind of parasite living inside your gecko. Several fecal tests or samples might also be required for

Chapter Nine: Common Illnesses of Crested Geckos

	geckos.		further treatment.
Swollen Joints	The main cause of swollen joint is excessive uric acid that is found in bloodstream. If there is too much uric acid, it usually develops into a salt crystal which then builds up in the joints.	Immobility, limping, swelling of joints/ limbs	Medications can only alleviate the pain but not necessarily stop it. You can however prevent it through proper husbandry. Your vet may also suggest cleaning or removing the affected joint to prevent it from spreading from other limb parts.

Chapter Nine: Common Illnesses of Crested Geckos

Egg Binding	This is another common mishap for breeding female crested geckos.	Symptoms include abdominal enlargement, loss of appetite, and difficulty in defecating.	Bring your pet to the vet immediately
Lung Infections	Also quite common among reptiles and crested geckos and is associated with the cage set up or perhaps improper husbandry.	Symptoms include breathing difficulties, formation of moisture around its nostrils, crusty eyes, whistling sound during breathing	Optimize the cage set up; ensure that the enclosure is set in the right temperature. Bring your pet to the vet for treatment.

Chapter Nine: Common Illnesses of Crested Geckos

Chapter Nine: Common Illnesses of Crested Geckos

Chapter Ten: Summary and Care Sheet

Keeping crested geckos are not just fun but also fulfilling especially if you're a true reptile hobbyist. They are very cute, they don't bite, they love to bond with their keepers, and they're very docile creatures. However, as you now have learned, keeping them can also be quite challenging. You need to ensure that you provide them with adequate care, feed them with the right foods, take them to the vet for a routine checkup, and most importantly keep their habitats clean and sanitary. All of this can contribute to the health and longevity of your pet gecko. This chapter will serve as your summary and care sheet so that you won't miss anything important.

Chapter Ten: Summary and Care Sheet

General Information

Pedigree: similar to a lizard species

Breed Size: quite small with a relatively long body structure

Length: adult length measures around 4 to 4.5 inches.

Weight: average weight for hatchlings are between 1 ½ grams to 2 grams; for juvenile average is 16 grams; for adult crested geckos average weight 30 to 50 grams (females); 25 grams to 35 grams (males).

Coat Texture: They have a unique appearance because their skin has fine and crested scales

Color: They are bred for various color patterns and morphs such as tans, yellows, oranges, red and other dark colors

Patterns/Markings: has a different pattern like black spots, harlequin, and tiger stripes.

Feet Type: Crested geckos, and geckos in general also possess double jointed toes which enables them to remove their food pad from the surface they're climbing into just by lifting their foot from the tip inward.

Temperament: docile, gentle, friendly, sensitive, delicate

Strangers: handling is not an issue as long as a person knows how to careful handle the gecko without restricting it or squeezing it

Chapter Ten: Summary and Care Sheet

Other Pets: can get along with other crested gecko breed with no more than one male in an enclosure. Not advisable to introduce to other house pets.

Exercise Needs: you just need to provide them with branches or perches to climb on since they are arboreal creatures.

Health Conditions: generally healthy but predisposed to common illnesses such as dehydration, Metabolic Bone Disease, respiratory problems, skin burns, impaction, egg binding, floppy tail syndrome, swollen joints, intestinal parasites and other diseases.

Lifespan: average 10 to 12 years; sometimes can last until 15 years or more

Morphs

Solid – Colored Crested Geckos (No pattern)

- Olive
- Yellow
- Buckskin
- Chocolate
- Near – black color
- Red
- Orange

Chapter Ten: Summary and Care Sheet

Tiger Crested Geckos: Tiger crested geckos also have the same solid – color but this time with stripes.

Flame Crested Geckos: Flame crested geckos can also possess any solid – based color though their dorsal is usually cream colored patterned with minimum pattern.

Harlequin Crested Geckos: Harlequins are crested geckos with high flame patterns.

Pinstripe Crested Geckos: Pinstripe pattern is a single and independent characteristic compared to a morph wherein there's a group of traits or specific patterns like flames, harlequin, or tiger.

Dalmatian Crested Gecko: Dalmatian spots in crested geckos are also considered as an independent trait just like pinstripe pattern.

White Spots Pattern: It appears as tiny white spots and is usually seen in the gecko's toes, belly, nose, and chest area.

Color Patterns

Creamsicle Crested Geckos: Creamsicle colored geckos have an orange flame pattern.

Blonde Crested Geckos: Its dark base color is contrasted with the creamy dorsal.

Chapter Ten: Summary and Care Sheet

Halloween Crested Geckos: These are harlequin patterned crested geckos that possess a dark near – black or orange colored markings.

Tricolor Crested Geckos: Tricolor crested geckos are basically harlequin geckos with 3 colors.

Mocha and Cream: Mocha crested geckos typically possess brown or tan colors with cream markings.

Cream on Cream: It's basically a light color with a cream dorsal and can often times be seen in tiger flamed patterned geckos.

Crested Geckos as Pets

Keeping One or More Crested Geckos

- Provide an adequate living environment
- As much as possible restrict in handling them if they're still young or if they just recently transferred to their new home.
- It is not recommended that you introduce them to other household pets.
- Try not to place more than one male crested gecko in an enclosure even if the cage is big. It will stress out the female geckos.
- Ensure that the enclosure is placed in a peaceful surrounding

Chapter Ten: Summary and Care Sheet

Expenses Overview

- Crested Gecko breed: $35 - $100
- Glass Enclosure with a screen top or lid: average of $89 - $100 (depending on size/ accessories included)
- Glass Enclosure (complete set with regulators/heaters): $200 - $300
- Bedding or Substrate: $6/bag
- Water Dish(for adults/large): $20
- Heaters/Misting Equipment: $50 and up
- Basking Lamp/UVB bulbs: $100 more or less
- Heat and Water Temperature Regulator/ Gauges: $5 and up
- Hiding Spots: $5
- Laying bin: $10 - $15
- Food: These are the sample prices of commercial food for crested geckos.

Pros and Cons of Keeping Crested Geckos

Pros

- Does not need too much attention
- Adaptability
- No exercise needed
- Small and easy to handle
- Have no special needs

Chapter Ten: Summary and Care Sheet

Cons

- Has quite a long lifespan (10 – 15 years)
- May come across as boring or non – interactive
- Cannot be handled or petted all the time
- May not be advisable for first time owners or young children

Acquiring Crested Geckos

Tips When Acquiring a Crested Gecko

- It is highly recommended that you only purchase a captive - bred crested gecko.
- Avoid buying from backyard breeders.
- It's also not recommended that you buy from pet stores
- You may opt for adoption
- Make sure that the species you're getting is the right breed of gecko.
- Purchase from legitimate breeders, crested gecko hobbyists, or during reptile conventions.
- As much as possible, don't purchase very young crested geckos.
- Quarantine your newly acquired pet.

Chapter Ten: Summary and Care Sheet

Tips When Choosing a Reputable Breeder

- Good breeders must be knowledgeable about the breeds.
- Breeders tend to know a lot about the species they breed so they must supply more specific information that you can't easily get online.
- Legit breeders know how to establish a good relationship with their potential/existing buyers.
- See how interested or proud the breeder is.
- Ensure that the breeder is someone who is approachable, and are open for mentorship.
- A reputable breeder will walk you through every step of the process.
- Know what to ask.

Tips When Choosing a Crested Gecko

- Check its health
- Notice any sort of illness or ill behavior.
- Have a checklist of your health standard.

Signs of Healthy Crested Geckos

Sign #1: Active and arboreal.

Sign #2: Balance and without any mobility disorders.

Chapter Ten: Summary and Care Sheet

Sign #3: Eyelash and fringe eyes.

Sign #4: Strong limbs.

Sign #5: Healthy skin and vibrant color.

Subject for Second Thoughts: Signs of an Unhealthy Crested Gecko

Sign #1: Inactive.

Sign #2: Eye problems.

Sign #3: Swollen limbs promoting mobility issues.

Sign #4: Uneven and unhealthy skin.

Sign #5: Other obvious health issues.

Housing Needs of Crested Geckos

Acclimating New Crested Geckos

- Ensure that the light bulb you're using is either a red/blue bulb with low light emissions.
- Use heat pads to provide a sort of belly heat for your crested geckos.

Chapter Ten: Summary and Care Sheet

- Ensure that the hiding place inside the enclosure is dark/ covered, warm, and just enough for their size to make them feel secure.
- You can handle them in the first 2 weeks but not too much
- Try feeding the same food that it was consuming at its breeder as dietary change can be quite stressful for them.
- Before adding another crested gecko in your collection, take time to quarantine it by putting the new creature in a separate enclosure for at least 30 – 45 days.
- Try not to place more than one male crested gecko in an enclosure even if the cage is big. It will stress out the female geckos.

Habitat Requirements

- Enclosure Size and Accessories
- The tank should preferably be 29 – gallon, and made out of solid glass. This is enough for 3 crested gecko adults.
- The enclosure should be secured so that your crested gecko won't be able to escape. Ensure that you have a metal mesh on top of the cage. It should be made out of metal mesh.

Chapter Ten: Summary and Care Sheet

- It's also advisable that you provide a hide house for your pet gecko. Ideally, it should be placed right over where the heat pads are located, and the under the heat lamp above the enclosure.
- When it comes to the substrate, it should be preferably made out of loose coconut fiber.

Heating and Lighting

- Adequate lighting like a 75 watt bulb heat, and under tank heaters or heat pads underneath will provide appropriate temperature and humidity levels inside your pet gecko's cage enclosure.
- You can turn on the UVB light for about 8 to 12 hours. That way they can get it along during their basking time.
- When it comes to heat lamps and other fixtures you can provide the tank with a basking area and a cooler area.
- You should ensure to turn on the heat lamp at day time, and turn it off at night time to create eight to twelve hours day/night cycle and not interrupt your pet gecko's sleeping pattern.

Chapter Ten: Summary and Care Sheet

Required Temperature

- An important note though, if ever the room temperature is below 70 degrees especially at night time, what you can do is provide a supplemental infrared light or a ceramic heat fixture.
- The humidity levels should be kept at 80%.

Housing Needs Checklist

- 29 – Gallon glass tank or vivarium that can suit 1 to 3 adult crested geckos
- Metal mesh on top (for security)
- Under Tank Heater or heat pads (should be place on the same side of the basking light)
- Hide house (place more than one if you have a few collections living in the same enclosure)
- Water bowl (big enough for your crested gecko/s)
- Heat bulbs
- Reptile Thermometer or humidity gauge (don't stick it inside the tank)
- Substrate (preferably coconut fiber)
- UVB bulb

Chapter Ten: Summary and Care Sheet

Nutrition for Your Crested Gecko

Commercial Gecko Diet (CGD)

- It is a powdered meal supplement that should be mixed with water to form a sort of paste that your crested gecko can easily digest. You can feed your crested gecko with the commercial diet daily or every other day.
- Most keepers use the Repashy Crested Gecko diet; this is a really simple diet mix and a lot of people also use it.
- The Pangea brand on the other hand is an expert in developing a varied diet for your crested gecko.

Fruits and Live Prey

- Crested geckos are omnivores which mean they both feed on live prey and organic food like fruits.
- Another thing you can feed your crested gecko as a treat is fruits such as mango, bananas, peach, papaya, apricots, fig, pear, strawberries, grapes and the likes.
- When feeding fruits what you can do is to mashed it up or cut it into little pieces so that your crested gecko can easily consume it.

Chapter Ten: Summary and Care Sheet

Protein and Supplements

- All live prey should be gut – loaded at least 24 hours before feeding it to your gecko.
- The supplements you're going to feed to your crickets/ locusts/ meal worms or other insects must have a good balance of vitamins and minerals that are targeted to meet your crested gecko's needs.
- It should also contain calcium and Vitamin D3, and must be of great quality.

How to Handle Your Crested Gecko

- Most crested geckos tolerate regular handling (after a few weeks adjusting to their new environment).
- When handling, you can let them jump from your hand to your other hand; let them hop freely and move your hand (or next obstacle) so they can easily target their next move. This can also serve as a form of exercise for them.
- Don't restrain or squeeze the crested gecko too hard because you can easily cut their tail off, and even stress them out.
- Another important thing to note when handling crested geckos is to make sure that your hands are clean before and after you handle them.

Chapter Ten: Summary and Care Sheet

Breeding Your Crested Geckos

Sexual Maturity and Sexual Dimorphism

- For females, most breeders recommend that you wait for your pet cresties to reach a certain weight; at least 40 to 50 grams for females, and minimum of 35 grams and above for males.

Breeding Requirements

- When it comes to the size of the enclosure, you may opt to buy an 18 x 18 x 18 cage for breeding pairs.
- If you plan on breeding 1 male cresty to 4 female crested geckos, you may need a slightly larger enclosure that measures about 18 x 18 x 24.
- It's ideal that you maximize the cage with a substantial amount of cage decors such as branches, leaves or live plants, hide house, and substrate as well as other needed requirements.

Breeding Basics

- The breeding season for crested geckos generally depends on where you live and also the average room temperature.

Chapter Ten: Summary and Care Sheet

- You can basically breed them all year round, and use the seasons in your state to your advantage.

- What you want to do is to give your female crested geckos at least 3 to 4 months rest after breeding it or after recently laying eggs so that they can recover from the whole process.

- Once they are ready to lay eggs, they'll just deposit it under the substrate and bury it.

- Crested geckos will lay an average of 6 to 10 clutches (2 eggs per clutch) every month or so though it can vary

- You should incubate the eggs from 70 to 84 degrees Fahrenheit. The longer you incubate them (say about 3 months), the more likely the baby crested gecko is larger and stronger.

- You may want to record the day the egg was laid, the incubation period, and the hatching day so that you can keep tab on the whole process. You need to document the breed pairs, the offspring, the laying period, how many clutches etc. so that you'll have a sort of history of the breed

Chapter Ten: Summary and Care Sheet

Common Illnesses of Crested Geckos

- Impaction
- Incomplete Skin Sloughing
- Dehydration
- Skin Burns
- Floppy – Tail Syndrome
- Metabolic Bone Disease (MBD)
- Fungal Dermatitis
- Intestinal Parasites
- Swollen Joints
- Egg Binding
- Lung Infections

Chapter Ten: Summary and Care Sheet

Glossary of Reptile Terms

Acrodont - having teeth that are anchored to the mandible (jaw bone) without individual sockets. Unique to certain orders of reptiles, including crested geckos.

Advanced Species - these species are best left to keepers with a number of years of experience with intermediate level geckos as they have unique husbandry requirements and limited numbers in captivity and possibly in the wild as well. They are very difficult to keep and even more so to breed.

Ambient Temperature - the average temperature of the room or area around the crested gecko that is unaffected by the basking light.

Arboreal - means "living in trees". The majority of crested gecko species fall into this category. These are species that spend most of their time in the middle to higher levels of the forest and rarely go to the ground aside from egg laying. They hunt, drink and mate in the branches of trees. Captive caging for arboreal animals should be taller than wide and include many branches to accommodate this lifestyle.

Aspirate - refers to inhaling liquid or food into the trachea, which can lead to choking, pneumonia, or death.

Bask - the full body absorption of heat from the sun, or overhead light source, by reptiles. It helps to regulate body temperature which in turn promotes proper digestion and a healthy metabolism.

Captive Bred (CB) - these animals have been bred, born and raised in captivity. They tend to be healthier and more hardy compared to WC/LTC specimens, as they are used to captive conditions and do not have heavy parasite burdens. Captive bred animals have also avoided the heavy stresses related to capture and exportation.

Captive Hatched (CH) - these are offspring from eggs hatched in captivity but were laid by a wild caught female who was gravid when imported. This also applies to babies born in captivity to a wild caught female.

Casque - French for 'helmet', the top of the head of all crested geckos is referred to as a casque.

Clutch - one group of eggs or the siblings that hatched from that one group.

Deworming - medical treatment of intestinal parasites diagnosed by a fecal exam.

Diapause - simulating a winter season by lowering temperatures for incubating eggs in the middle segment of incubation. It is required by some species.

Dripper - a vessel that allows water to drip down into the cage for the crested gecko to drink. May be as simple a hole in the bottom of a cup, or commercially produced product like the "Little Dripper".

Dusting - applying a powdered vitamin or mineral supplement to feeder insects immediately before feeding them to a crested gecko.

Dysecdysis - a problem with shedding that result in retained skin that should have fallen off and may cause additional problems such as appendage stricture. Usually results from improper temperature and humidity parameters.

Ectotherm - an animal that controls body temperature through external means since it cannot generate its own body heat (cold-blooded).

Edema - an accumulation of fluid under the skin, usually in the gular region, suspected to be caused by vitamin imbalance or organ failure.

Eggbound - a serious condition for female egg laying crested geckos where for medical, nutritional or environmental reasons they are unable to lay their eggs. Fatal if not treated.

Expert Species - these are species left only for the most experienced keepers, as they are challenging in all aspects. These crested geckos are also highly limited in their captive population due to their care needs and may be endangered or threatened in their natural habitat. They are nearly impossible to breed. Ex: Parsons

Farm Raised (FR) - this term can imply different things depending on the source, and resellers may label these animals CB or WC, depending on the personal opinion of the reseller and what is more profitable. These animals typically need the medical care of WCs, but tend to be somewhat better adapted to captive conditions than WC animals.

Fecal - generally refers to diagnostic testing of a fresh fecal (poop) sample for the presence of microscopic eggs of intestinal parasites performed by a vet.

Gout - a medical condition often recognized by swollen, painful joints caused by crystallization of uric acid crystals within the joints. This has been associated with excessive dietary protein, chronic dehydration, imbalance of calcium, phosphorus, vitamin A, vitamin D and/or kidney disease. This is a very painful disease and there is not an effective treatment.

Gravid - carrying eggs, or pregnant in the case of live-bearing species.

Gular - the region under the neck just in front of the arms.

Gutloading - providing a healthy balanced diet high in calcium to feeder insects before feeding them to the crested gecko so that the nutrients are passed to the crested gecko.

Hemipenes - paired reproductive organ of male lizards in the order Squamata, like crested geckos.

Husbandry - the practice of creating a proper captive environment and maintaining appropriate humidity, temperature, lighting, good nutrition, etc.

Impaction - intestines are clogged (impacted) with a non-digestible material, such as dirt, bark, rocks, excessive chitin, etc that prevents the digestion and passage of food. May be life-threatening if not treated.

Intermediate Species - these species are for more experienced keepers, having some unique husbandry requirements challenging enough that experience in general care of crested geckos is recommended before attempting.

Lethargy - decrease in activity or sleeping more than usual, often associated with signs of illness.

Litter - the group of siblings from an viviparous species.

Locale - a natural geographic location that represents specific color variation within the same species, usually the result of geographic isolation. Panther crested geckos are commonly labeled by locale. The panther locales are named after geographic areas in Madagascar and each represents a unique color pattern. For example: Nosy Be crested geckos are generally very blue and come from an island off Madagascar called Nosy Be.

Long Term Captive (LTC) - these are animals that have been in captivity over 8-12 months but were originally wild caught. They have usually adapted to captivity at this point, and are more stable at this stage than when originally imported since common health issues have been resolved.

MBD (metabolic bone disease) - condition of weak bones that break easily and overall metabolic illness due to lack of dietary calcium, imbalanced nutrition and/or lack of UVB rays. Serious problem leaving to permanent damage and death if not addressed quickly.

Montane - crested gecko species existing in a more mountainous environment at higher altitudes, lower temperatures and higher relative humidity than traditional tropical species.

Morph - refers to the color pattern variations of crested geckos within one species established by selective breeding in captivity for a particular trait. For example: translucent veiled crested geckos.

Mouthrot (stomatitis) - an infection of the mouth that could be deep into the underlying bone and can spread to the rest of the body. Requires veterinary attention and antibiotics specific to the bacteria causing the infection.

Novice Species - crested geckos in general are not beginner animals but those designated "novice" are considered the best "beginner" species in the hobby with large, stable captive populations relative to other species. They are relatively easy to breed as well. Examples: panther and veiled crested geckos

Oviparous - mode of reproduction where embryos develop inside eggs that have been laid by the mother. Little to no development occurs inside the mother's body (ie., birds and most crested gecko species).

Ovoviviparous - this mode of reproduction is not found in crested geckos.

Parietal Eye - a photoreceptive (able to sense light) scale on the top of the head that can sense light when the eyes are closed and may play a part in regulating circadian rhythm and hormone production for thermoregulation.

Prolapse - internal organ that has inverted on itself and protruded out of the body through the vent. A medical emergency that should be addressed asap.

Receptive - referring to a female being willing to breed with a male, often indicated by a distinct change in coloration depending on the species.

Rostral process - the crest of scales at the tip of the nose.

Shed (ecdysis) - the periodic shedding of the outer layer of skin in reptiles to allow for growth. Becomes less frequent as the reptile gets older.

Supplements - concentrated calcium or vitamins, usually in powdered form, to add value to the diet.

Tarsal Spur - a bump on the back of the hind feet of some species of crested geckos. Only present on males.

Terrestrial - these are species that in the wild reside on the ground or in the lowest levels of the forest, like shrubbery, with some time spent on the ground. In captivity these species may take advantage of available height, but floorspace should be considered when designing housing. Very few crested geckos fall into this category - mostly pygmy species.

Turret - the mobile portion of the eyeball covered in skin around the visible eye opening.

Urates - the white portion of the feces that is essentially concentrated urine. Yellow or orange color indicates dehydration.

Upper Respiratory Infection (URI) - an infection of the nasal cavity, trachea, and/or bronchi that manifests as lethargy, wheezing or popping noises while breathing and excess saliva in the mouth.

UVB - invisible ultraviolet rays emitted by the sun with a spectrum between 280-315nm, responsible for vitamin D synthesis in the skin to regulate calcium homeostasis. It is critical to crested gecko health.

Vent - common opening for the digestive, urinary and reproductive tract in birds and reptiles just under the base of the tail.

Vivarium - Latin for "place of life", a cage attempting to recreate the natural environment of the animal's native habitat.

Viviparous - mode of reproduction where embryos develop inside the mother's body until they are ready to be born, at which point the mother gives birth to live young that immediately break free of a membrane.

Wild Caught (WC) - these are animals collected in the wild and exported from their native country - usually young adults. They will probably need to be treated for parasites and other medical conditions like dehydration, are much stressed, and may come in in very bad condition. They are best left for keepers with more experience, even if the species is considered Novice, for these reasons.

Zygodactyl feet - The arrangement of toes on the hands and feet where the 2nd and 4th digits point forward while the

1st and 3rd digits point backward. It is a misnomer that crested geckos are zygodactyl. They actually have 5 digits fused into two groups on each foot. Their toe arrangement also alternates between front and hind limbs

Index

A

antibiotics 109. 110. 111. 112
appearance 3, 11, 15, 41, 111
attention 77, 78, 87

B

black 6, 8, 21, 116
body 6, 13, 14, 21, 22, 50, 70, 76, 77, 79, 80, 85, 90, 92, 110, 112
breeder 30, 37, 40, 41, 42, 43, 44, 45, 47, 48, 51, 53, 62, 86, 89, 92, 102
breeding 1, 10, 13, 15, 33, 41, 43, 85
brown 6, 29, 69, 116
brushy 24, 117

C

capable 7, 17, 22
captivity 6, 24, 32, 35, 63, 101, 103, 110,
captured 6, 17
care 1, 3, 5, 25, 28, 30, 36, 40
choosing 7, 40, 45, 62
colors 5, 6, 28, 41, 81
companion 7, 30, 121
contrasting 6
covers 8

D

dark	6, 21, 61, 65, 81, 105
delivery	17
diet	9, 42
different	5, 11, 21, 24, 31, 52, 65, 69
divided	17
docile	3, 5, 113
dusk	20

E

eggs	15, 21, 23, 24, 32, 73
embryo	22, 97
externally	21
eye	25, 59, 67, 76, 116

F

fact	15, 30, 32, 70, 73
family	14, 18, 20, 22
feature	17
feed	18, 27, 32, 37, 38
feet	14, 15, 32, 125
finish	18
found	14, 30, 31 33, 106
fun	82

G

generations	98

genes 21
gland 21, 24, 25, 116

H

home 59, 74, 104

I

illegally 15
interactions 15
interesting 15, 30

J

jail. 44

K

kick 13

L

large 14, 25, 26, 70, 73, 76
lid. 14, 97
little 13, 77, 78
live 71, 72, 73, 76, 77, 79

M

make	101
melanin	17
modified	17, 21
mouth	18, 23, 26

N

natured	15
new	41, 63, 82
North	14, 33, 112,
novel	15

O

outline	16, 125

P

patterns	14, 15, 100
personalities	14
physical	19, 75
predators	16, 69, 84
prep	13
popular	14, 105, 108

R

requirements	36, 37, 39, 74, 104

S

sign 67, 115, 120
skilled..15

T

threatened 90, 92, 117

Photo Credits

Page Photo by user Chris Parker via Flickr.com,

https://www.flickr.com/photos/chrisparker2012/14030094081/

Page Photo by user Josh More via Flickr.com,

https://www.flickr.com/photos/guppiecat/9351678626/

Page Photo by user Florence Ivy via Flickr.com,

https://www.flickr.com/photos/amalthea23/26564084105/

Page Photo by user Lush Design via Flickr.com,

https://www.flickr.com/photos/lush-design/5543374585/

Page Photo by user John via Flickr.com,

https://www.flickr.com/photos/8373783@N07/2908575008/in/photostream/

Page Photo by user Lush Design via Flickr.com,

https://www.flickr.com/photos/lush-design/5543397389/

Page Photo by user Hehaden via Flickr.com,

https://www.flickr.com/photos/hellie55/22793282953/

Page Photo by user Jennifer Morrow via Flickr.com,

https://www.flickr.com/photos/donotlick/4509613924/

Page Photo by user Austin Valley via Flickr.com,

https://www.flickr.com/photos/austinvalley/5689323540/

Page Photo by user Florence Ivy via Flickr.com,

https://www.flickr.com/photos/amalthea23/34502511212/

Page Photo by user Tom Lee via Flickr.com,

https://www.flickr.com/photos/68942208@N02/23377451836/

References

Care of Crested Geckos – The Spruce

https://www.thespruce.com/care-of-crested-geckos-1238764

Care Sheet for Crested Geckos – DFWHerp.org

http://www.dfwherp.org/Caresheet-Crested.pdf

Crested Gecko – Wikipedia.org

https://en.wikipedia.org/wiki/Crested_gecko

Crested Gecko – DrsFosterSmith.com

https://www.drsfostersmith.com/pic/article.cfm?articleid=2499

Crested Gecko and Gargoyle Gecko Care Information – CreestedGecko.com

http://www.crestedgecko.com/CrestedGeckoandGargoyleGeckoCareInformation.pdf

Crested Gecko Care Sheet – ReptilesMagazine.com

http://www.reptilesmagazine.com/Care-Sheets/Lizards/Crested-Gecko/

Crested Gecko Care Sheet – PetDepot.net

https://petdepot.net/care_sheets/Crested_Gecko_care_sheet.pdf

Crested Gecko Care Sheet: Rhacodactylus ciliates – StickyLizards.com

http://www.stickylizards.com/images/care_sheet.pdf

Crested Gecko (Rhacodactylus ciliatus) Caresheet – ThePetCabin.co.uk

http://www.thepetcabin.co.uk/files/8013/1417/1414/crested_gecko.pdf

Morphs and Colors - MoonValleyReptiles.com

http://www.moonvalleyreptiles.com/crested-geckos/morphs

The Crested Gecko in Captivity – Coroflot.com

http://s3images.coroflot.com/user_files/individual_files/413631_xERa_eiQoWSLrBEyLuoKDdqnV.pdf

What You Need To Know about Crested Geckos – AmazonAws.com

https://s3-eu-west-1.amazonaws.com/peregrine-download/Care+Sheets/crested-gecko-care-sheet-a4-v1-SMF.pdf

www.ingramcontent.com/pod-product-compliance
Lightning Source LLC
LaVergne TN
LVHW051839080426
835512LV00018B/2974